A Dog Named Bear

This is my story to share

Debbie Hauser

Debbie Hauser
A Dog Named Bear

Published by Spines
ISBN: 979-8-89383-590-8

Dedicated to the people who open their hearts
and lives to homeless animals

"I believe that storytelling is the most successful way of
helping people understand the true nature of animals"

Jane Goodall

My name is Bear.
I used to live at a shelter for homeless animals.
I was very sad. Had I done something bad?

Then one day- Oh wait, can it be?
These humans are looking at me!

They are holding a puppy and she is
the color of ginger. She is quite spunky!

OH HAPPY DAY- I HAVE A FAMILY!

On the weekends we love to ride in the car to The Cottage. It is not so far.

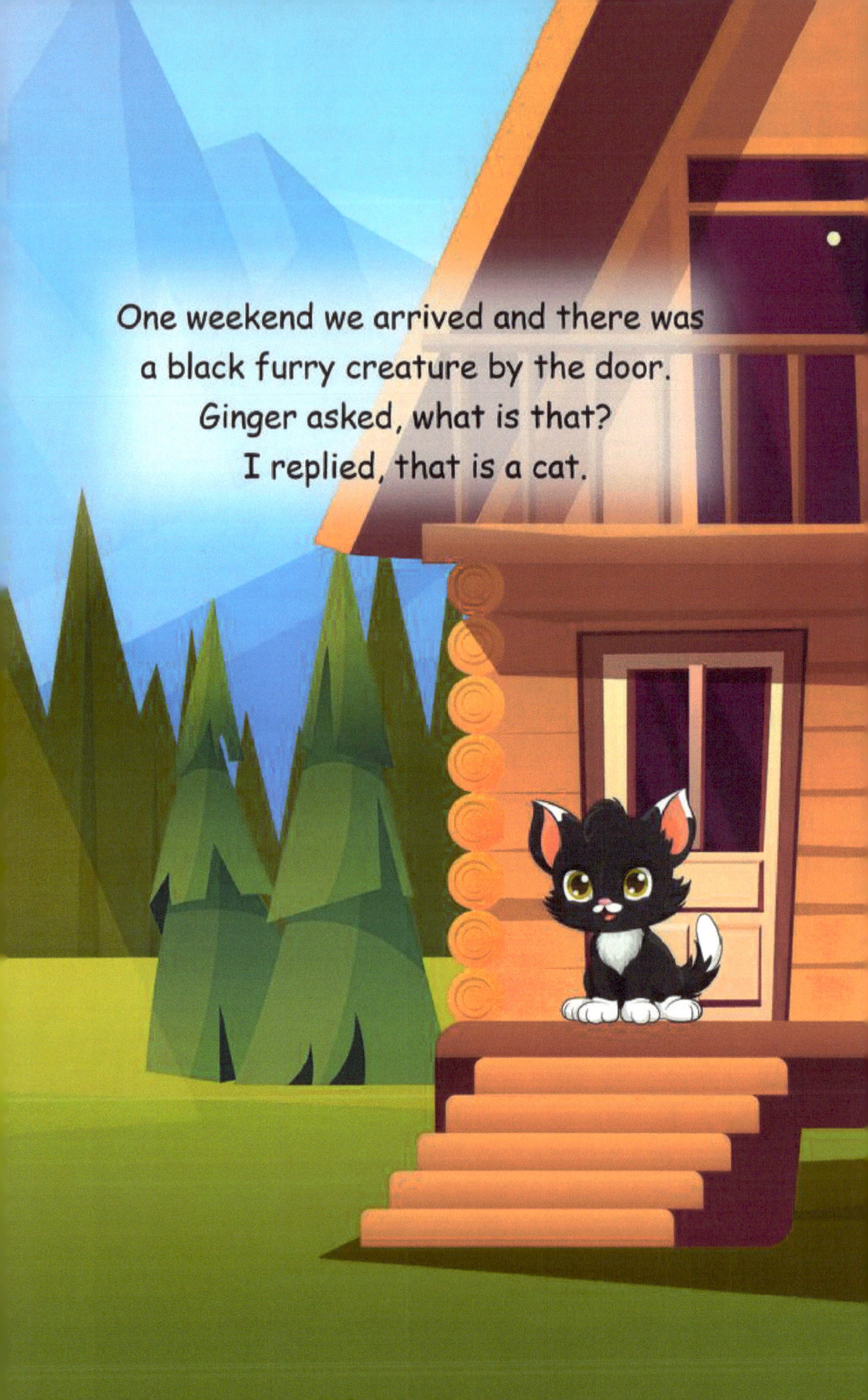
One weekend we arrived and there was
a black furry creature by the door.
Ginger asked, what is that?
I replied, that is a cat.

Ginger said, he does not bark and
he does not go for walks.
Does he talk? Why is he here?

I replied, the cat is here because he needed a home. His name is Boots. He has his own language but if you listen carefully, you will manage.

Ginger said, I see that he is
furry with 4 legs and a tail, like us.
But I am not sure if we can be friends.
Will Boots always be little?

I replied, yes Boots will always be little so we must be kind and careful. I reached out my paw to him, "Don't worry little Boots, I will watch out for you. We two will be friends."

Ginger said, that is all fine and good, because
I have discovered how much I like cat food!

Boots likes to go outside. It is my job to
watch out for him. Sometimes he is hard to find.
But I look up and wag my tail.
There he is way up in a tree!

At the cottage we see our friends David and Diane.
They give us lots of treats.
And Ginger always finds Boots' food to eat!

Sometimes our humans go away.
Ginger and I are sad, but then
Aunt Nancy comes, and saves the day!

Ginger and I love to go on walks.
One day she said, my leg hurts and
I cannot go with you.
Will I ever be able to go on walks
with you again?

I said, yes you can! I have a plan.
Just sit in this Red Flyer wagon,
Red Flyer

and I will help pull it with you in it.

Because of her leg,
Ginger went to the doctor's office, and
I went with her. It is a scary experience,
but always better with a friend.

Dr. Lambarri said,
"Ginger is on the mend. Soon you will all be
able to walk together again!"

ABOUT THE AUTHOR

Debbie Hauser is a passionate writer in the field of pets and dogs. With a unique ability to communicate with animals, she shares heartwarming stories of adopted rescue animals. Her empathy for animals shines through in her writing, inspired by her own experiences with dogs, horses, and other rescued creatures.

www.ingramcontent.com/pod-product-compliance
Lightning Source LLC
Chambersburg PA
CBHW040905110726
48005CB00001B/202